PRAYERS

■ DURING THE ■

NIGHT

LITURGY
TRAINING
PUBLICATIONS

ACKNOWLEDGMENTS

We are grateful to the many publishers and authors who have given permission to include their work. Every effort has been made to determine the ownership of all texts and to make proper arrangements for their use. We will gladly correct in future editions any oversight or error that is brought to our attention.

Unless otherwise noted, excerpts from scripture are from the *New Revised Standard Version* of the Bible © 1989, Division of Christian Education of the National Council of the Churches of Christ in the United States of America. Used by permission. All rights reserved.

Scripture on pp. 2, 16, 21, 26, 28 and 39–40 are from the *New American Bible with Revised New Testament and Psalms,* copyright © 1991, 1986, 1978 Confraternity of Christian Doctrine, Inc., Washington, D.C. Used with permission. All rights reserved. No portion of the *New American Bible* may be reproduced by any means without permission in writing by the copyrighted owner.

Acknowledgments continued on page 57.

PRAYERS DURING THE NIGHT © 2003 Archdiocese of Chicago: Liturgy Training Publications, 1800 North Hermitage Avenue, Chicago IL 60622-1101; 1-800-933-1800, fax 1-800-933-7094, e-mail orders@ltp.org. All rights reserved. See our website at www.ltp.org.

This book was compiled by Kathleen Spears Hopkins and edited by Lorie Simmons with assistance from Margaret Brennan and Laura Goodman. Carol Mycio was the production editor. Typesetting was done by Anne Fritzinger in Galliard. Cover art is by Jean Troxel. The photos in the art on pages 1, 14, 27 and 41 © 2003 www.clipart.com.

Printed in the United States of America.

Library of Congress Control Number: 2003101413

1-56854-452-9

PDNITE

FOREWORD

Speak the word *night,* and a flood of images streams forth: darkness, danger, quiet, peace, fear, calm, worry, sleep, wakefulness, watching. Before the industrial age brought bright light to every hour of the day, the coming of darkness signaled the end of work and activity and the beginning of quiet and rest. Darkness allows evil its cover and holiness its root-room for growth. Poets and saints have found night a privileged time for prayer and meditation, and a powerful image for the struggle for holiness which calls forth the soul into relationship with God. The image of the "Dark Night of the Soul," so often misunderstood, is the period of purgation and purification of the soul, which prepares it for union with God.

Poets, saints and ordinary people have feared and loved the night, praying for deliverance from its perils and savoring its sheltering solitude. They have blessed the darkness and filled it with words of longing for the presence of God.

This little book offers prayers and reflections from scripture, from the liturgy of the church, from the writings of poets, saints and ordinary people of different countries and religious traditions. May they deepen the holiness of your nights, whether you wake or sleep.

—*Kathleen Spears Hopkins*

Shadows fall,
  but hope, prevailing,
calms every fear.

As Daylight Fades

Then God said: "Let there be lights in the dome of the sky, to separate day from night. Let them mark the fixed times, the days and the years, and serve as luminaries in the dome of the sky, to shed light upon the earth." And so it happened: God made the two great lights, the greater one to govern the day, and the lesser one to govern the night; and he made the stars. God set them in the dome of the sky, to shed light upon the earth, to govern the day and the night, and to separate the light from the darkness. God saw how good it was.

—*Genesis 1:14–18*

Day is done, but Love unfailing
dwells ever here;
shadows fall, but hope, prevailing,
calms every fear.

Loving Father, none forsaking,
take our hearts, of Love's own making,
watch our sleeping, guard our waking,
be always near!

Dark descends, but Light unending
shines through our night;
you are with us, ever lending
new strength to sight;
one in love, your truth confessing,
one in hope of heaven's blessing,
may we see, in love's possessing,
love's endless light!

Eyes will close, but you, unsleeping,
watch by our side;
death may come in Love's safe keeping
still we abide.
God of love, all evil quelling,
sin forgiving, fear dispelling,
stay with us, our hearts indwelling,
this eventide!

—*James Quinn*

O Lord, support us all the day long, until the shadows lengthen, and the evening comes, and the busy world is hushed, and the fever of life is over, and our work is done. Then in *thy* mercy, grant us a safe lodging, and a holy rest, and peace at the last.

—*Book of Common Prayer*

"Come to me, all you that are weary and are carrying heavy burdens, and I will give you rest. Take my yoke upon you, and learn from me; for I am gentle and humble in heart, and you will find rest for your souls. For my yoke is easy, and my burden is light."

—*Matthew 11:28–30*

I confess to almighty God,
and to you, my brothers and sisters,
that I have sinned through my own fault
in my thoughts and in my words,
in what I have done,
and in what I have failed to do;
and I ask blessed Mary, ever virgin,
all the angels and saints,
and you, my brothers and sisters,
to pray for me to the Lord our God.

—*Roman Missal*

O LORD, my heart is not lifted up,
    my eyes are not raised too high;
I do not occupy myself with things
    too great and too marvelous for me.
But I have calmed and quieted my soul,
    like a weaned child with its mother;
    my soul is like the weaned child that is
        with me.

O Israel, hope in the LORD
    from this time on and forevermore.

—*Psalm 131*

In the Name of God, the merciful Lord
     of mercy.
Praise be to God, the Lord of all being,
the merciful Lord of mercy,
Master of the day of judgement.
You alone we serve: to You alone we come
     for aid.
Guide us in the straight path,
The path of those whom You have blessed,
not of those against whom there is displeasure,
nor of those who go astray.

    —*the Fātihah (the first passage of the Qur'an) prayed*
      in Arabic during the five prayer times Muslims
      observe daily, including sunset prayer.

Take my tired body, my confused mind, and my restless soul into your arms and give me rest, simple quiet rest. Do I ask too much too soon? I should not worry about that. You will let me know. Come, Lord Jesus, come.

—*Henri J. M. Nouwen, twentieth century*

O God, you have let me pass this day in peace,
let me pass the night in peace
O Lord who has no Lord,
there is no strength but in thee.
Thou alone hast no obligation.
Under thy hand I pass the night.
Thou art my mother and my father.

—*evening prayer from Kenya*

I am placing my soul and my body
On Thy sanctuary this night, O God,
On Thy sanctuary, O Jesus Christ,
On Thy sanctuary, O Spirit of perfect truth,
    The Three who would defend my cause,
    Nor turn Their backs upon me.

Thou, Father, who art kind and just,
Thou, Son, who didst overcome death,
Thou, Holy Spirit of power,
Be keeping me this night from harm;
    The Three who would justify me
    Keeping me this night and always.

—*Carmina Gadelica*

Grant that we may lie down in peace, Eternal God, and raise us up, O Sovereign, to life renewed. Spread over us the shelter of Your peace; guide us with Your good counsel; and for Your name's sake, be our Help.

Shield us from hatred and plague; keep us from war and famine and anguish; subdue our inclination to evil. O God, our Guardian and Helper, our gracious and merciful Sovereign, give us refuge in the shadow of Your wings. O guard our coming and our going, that now and always we have life and peace.

—*the Hashkiveinu, traditional Jewish evening prayer*

Keep watch, dear Lord,
with those who work or watch
or weep this night,
and give your angels charge over those
      who sleep.

Tend the sick, Lord Christ;
give rest to the weary,
bless the dying,
soothe the suffering,
pity the afflicted,
shield the joyous;
and all for your love's sake.

—*Book of Common Worship*

God shield the house, the fire, the kine,
Every one who dwells herein to-night.
Shield myself and my beloved group,
Preserve us from violence and from harm;
Preserve us from foes this night,
For the sake of the Son of the Mary Mother,
In this place, and in every place wherein they
        dwell to-night,
On this night and on every night,
    This night and every night.

—*Carmina Gadelica*

O Lord, Jesus Christ,
who art as the shadow of a great rock
    in a weary land,
who beholdest thy weak creatures
weary of labour, weary of pleasure,
weary of hope deferred, weary of self;
in thine abundant compassion,
and fellow feeling with us,
and unutterable tenderness,
bring us, we pray thee,
unto thy rest.

—*Christina Rossetti, nineteenth century*

Into your hands, Lord, I commend my spirit.

—*Liturgy of the Hours*

May the all-powerful Lord grant us
    a restful night
and a peaceful death.

Protect us, Lord, as we stay awake;
watch over us as we sleep,
that awake, we may keep watch
    with Christ,
and asleep, rest in his peace.

—*from Night Prayer, Liturgy of the Hours*

Lord Jesus Christ, as daylight fades,
As shine the lights of eventide,
We praise the Father with the Son,
The Spirit blest and with them one.

—*Phos Hilaron, Greek, third century*

Deep peace of the
Shining Stars
to you.

THE DARK, TOO, BLOOMS
AND SINGS

The pleated lampshade, slightly askew,
dust a silverish muting of the lamp's fake brass.
My sock-monkey on the pillow,
    tail and limbs asprawl,
weary after a day of watching sunlight
    prowl the house like a wolf.
Gleams of water in my bedside glass.
Miraculous water, so peacefully
waiting to be consumed.

The day's crowding arrived
at this abundant stillness. Each thing
given to the eye before sleep, and water
at my lips before darkness. Gift after gift.

—*Denise Levertov*

Bless the LORD, my soul!
　　LORD, my God, you are great indeed!
You made the moon to mark the seasons,
　　the sun that knows the hour of its setting.
You bring darkness and night falls,
　　then all the beasts of the forest roam abroad.
Young lions roar for prey;
　　they seek their food from God.
When the sun rises, they steal away
　　and rest in their dens.
People go forth to their work,
　　to their labor till evening falls.

—*Psalm 104:1, 19–23*

Eighty-eight thousand six-hundred
different species in North America.
　　In the trees, the grasses
around us. Maybe more, maybe
several million on each acre of earth. This one
as well as any other. Where you are standing
at dusk. Where the moon
appears to be climbing the eastern sky.

Where the wind
seems to be traveling through the trees,
         and the frogs
are content in their black ponds or else
why do they sing? Where you feel
a power that is not you but flows
into you like a river. Where you lie down
         and breathe
the sweet honey of the grass and count
the stars; where you fall asleep listening
to the simple chords repeated, repeated.
Where, resting, you feel
the perfection, the rising, the happiness
of their dark wings.

—*Mary Oliver*

Then the mystery was revealed to Daniel in a
vision of the night, and Daniel blessed the God
of heaven.

—*Daniel 2:19*

Deep peace of the Running Wave to you.
Deep peace of the Flowing Air to you.
Deep peace of the Quiet Earth to you.
Deep peace of the Shining Stars to you.
Deep peace of the Son of Peace to you.

—*Celtic Benediction*

Charm with your stainlessness
    these winter nights,
Skies, and be perfect!
Fly vivider in the fiery dark, you quiet meteors,
And disappear.
You moon, be slow to go down,
This is your full!

The four white roads make off in silence
Towards the four parts of the starry universe.
Time falls like manna at the corners
    of the wintry earth.
We have become more humble than the rocks,
More wakeful than the patient hills.

Charm with your stainlessness these nights
        in Advent, holy spheres,
While minds, as meek as beasts,
Stay close at home in the sweet hay;
And intellects are quieter than the flocks
        that feed by starlight.

Oh pour your darkness and your brightness
        over all our solemn valleys,
You skies: and travel like the gentle Virgin,
Toward the planets' stately setting,
Oh white full moon as quiet as Bethlehem!

—*Thomas Merton, twentieth century*

God of midnight's deepest silence
and heaven's brightest glory,
whose radiant majesty angelic choirs praise
and whose hidden glory lowly shepherds adore,
your grace has appeared, bringing salvation
        to all,
in a child wrapped in swaddling clothes
and lying in a manger.

Upon the deep darkness of our world
shine the light of your countenance
that our hearts may exult and sing for joy
at the Savior's coming,
with angels and shepherds, with Mary
        and Joseph,
and with all people of good will
who long for your peace.

We ask this through our Lord Jesus Christ,
Emmanuel, God with us,
your Son who lives and reigns with you
in the unity of the Holy Spirit,
God for ever and ever.

—*Peter J. Scagnelli*

Praise the LORD, who is so good;
    God's love endures forever;
Who alone has done great wonders,
    God's love endures forever;
Who skillfully made the heavens,
    God's love endures forever;
Who spread the earth upon the waters,
    God's love endures forever;
Who made the great lights,
    God's love endures forever;
The moon and stars to rule the night,
    God's love endures forever.
Praise the God of heaven,
    God's love endures forever.

—*Psalm 136:1, 4–7, 9, 26*

At the end of four hundred thirty years, on
that very day, all the companies of the LORD
went out from the land of Egypt. That was for
the LORD a night of vigil, to bring them out
of the land of Egypt. That same night is a vigil
to be kept for the LORD by all the Israelites
throughout their generations.

—*Exodus 12:41–42*

This is the night
when first you set the children of Israel free:
you saved our ancestors from slavery in Egypt
and led them dry-shod through the sea.

This is the night
when Jesus Christ broke the chains of death
and in triumphant glory rose from the grave.
A night to restore lost innocence
        and bring mourners joy!
A night to cast out hatred!
A night for seeking peace and humbling pride!

O truly blessed night
when heaven is wedded to earth
and we are reconciled with God!

—*from the Exultet, the Easter Vigil, Roman Missal*

For the cloud of the LORD was on the
tabernacle by day, and fire was in the cloud by
night, before the eyes of all the house of Israel
at each stage of their journey.

—*Exodus 40:38*

Lord of light
help me to know
that you are also
Lord of night.
And by your choice
when all is dark
and still and stark
you use your voice.

—*Harry Alfred Wiggett*

To go in the dark with a light is to know
      the light.
To know the dark, go dark. Go without sight,
and find that the dark, too, blooms and sings,
and is traveled by dark feet and dark wings.

    —*Wendell Berry*

You darkness, that I come from,
I love you more than all the fires
that fence in the world,
for the fire makes
a circle of light for everyone,
and then no one outside learns of you.

But the darkness pulls in everything:
shapes and fires, animals and myself,
how easily it gathers them!—
powers and people—
and it is possible a great energy
is moving near me.
I have faith in nights.

    —*Rainer Maria Rilke, twentieth century*

Come, Lord,
and cover me with the night.
Spread your grace over us
as you assured us you would do.

Your promises are more than
all the stars in the sky;
your mercy is deeper than the night.
Lord, it will be cold.
The night comes with its breath of death.
Night comes; the end comes; you come.

Lord, we wait for you
day and night.

—*night prayer from Ghana*

Lord Jesus, you are the centre towards which all things are moving: if it be possible, make a place for us all in the company of those elect and holy ones whom your loving care has liberated one by one from the chaos of our present existence and who now are being slowly incorporated into you in the unity of the new earth.

—*Pierre Teilhard de Chardin, twentieth century*

All you hosts of the Lord, bless the Lord;
    praise and exalt him above all forever.
Sun and moon, bless the Lord;
    praise and exalt him above all forever.
Stars of heaven, bless the Lord;
    praise and exalt him above all forever.
Nights and days, bless the Lord;
    praise and exalt him above all forever.
Light and darkness, bless the Lord;
    praise and exalt him above all forever.

—*Daniel 3:61–63, 71–72*

Lighten our darkness, Lord, we pray.

FEARFUL DARK

Darkness we know too well: the toddler's plea
that the night-light be left on, the grandpa's
terror that he might go blind, the growing
depression of the community after days of gray
rain or winter's early nightfall. Into such
darkness threatening to overwhelm the world
comes Christ our light, reversing human fact
with divine truth.

—*Gail Ramshaw*

My eyes cannot close in sleep;
    I am troubled and cannot speak.
I consider the days of old;
    the years long past I remember.
In the night I meditate in my heart;
    I ponder and my spirit broods.

—*Psalm 77:5–7*

Amid thoughts from visions of the night,
    when deep sleep falls on mortals,
dread came upon me, and trembling,
    which made all my bones shake.

    —Job 4:13–14

Lord,
this winter night
I have sharpened myself
like a bookkeeper's pencil
bent over random entries.

This winter night
there will be no balance.
The fragments of memory
will not be pieced into a story.
The days are so themselves
they will not gather into weeks.
Each moment is alien to every other,
a life of blazing fireworks,
beautiful and gone,
extinguished in the black and trackless sky.

This winter night
truth will have its way.
I will remain cluttered
like my desk—
beneath a book I've never read
a year-old phone number
of someone I've forgotten.
It will remain a runaway life
with the reins beyond reach
and the rider's eyes blasted into amazement
by the winds of tomorrow.

—*John Shea*

O LORD, you have searched me and known me.
You know when I sit down and when I rise up;
    you discern my thoughts from far away.
You search out my path and my lying down,
    and are acquainted with all my ways.

Where can I go from your spirit?
　　Or where can I flee from your presence?
If I ascend to heaven, you are there;
　　if I make my bed in Sheol, you are there.

If I say, "Surely the darkness shall cover me,
　　and the light around me become night,"
even the darkness is not dark to you;
　　the night is as bright as the day,
　　for darkness is as light to you.

—*Psalm 139:1–3, 7–8, 11–12*

Take my hand, Precious Lord,
Lead me on, let me stand.
I am tired, I am weak, I am worn.
Through the storm, through the night,
　　lead me on to the light.
Take my hand, Precious Lord, lead me home.

When my way grows drear, Precious Lord,
    linger near
When my life is almost gone.
Hear my cry, hear my call, hold my hand,
    lest I fall.
Take my hand, Precious Lord, lead me home.

When the darkness appears and the night
    draws near
And the day is past and gone,
At the river I stand,
Guide my feet, hold my hand.
Take my hand, Precious Lord, lead me home.

—Thomas A. Dorsey, twentieth century

A man is lying on a bed
in a small room in the dark.
Weary and afraid, he prays
for courage to sleep, to wake
and work again; he doubts
that waking when he wakes
will recompense his sleep.

His prayers lean upward
on the dark and fall
like flares from a catastrophe.
He is a man breathing the fear
of hopeless prayer, prayed
in hope. He breathes the prayer
of his fear that gives a light
by which he sees only himself lying
in the dark, a low mound asking
almost nothing at all.
And then, long yet before dawn,
comes what he had not thought:
love that causes him to stir
like the dead in the grave, being
remembered—his own love or
Heaven's, he does not know.
But now it is all around him;
it comes down upon him
like a summer rain falling
slowly, quietly in the dark.

—*Wendell Berry*

Lighten our darkness, Lord, we pray; and in your mercy defend us from all perils and dangers of this night; for the love of your only Son, our Saviour Jesus Christ.

—*Gelasian Sacramentary*

I said, feeling helpless, that maybe I could read her the best bedtime story I knew. She smiled faintly and said that she would like that. So I read Psalm 4 aloud, catching my breath at the last lines: "I will lie down and sleep comes at once, for you, alone, Lord, make me dwell in safety." We both wept, and were able to sleep a little, before the empty dawn.

—*Kathleen Norris*

When I call, answer me, O God of justice;
from anguish you released me, have mercy and
      hear me!

You rebels, how long will your hearts be closed,
will you love what is futile and seek what is false?

It is the LORD who grants favors to those who
    are merciful;
the LORD hears me whenever I call.

Tremble; do not sin: ponder on your bed and
    be still.
Make justice your sacrifice and trust
    in the LORD.

"What can bring us happiness?" many say.
Lift up the light of your face on us, O LORD.

You have put into my heart a greater joy
than they have from abundance of corn and
    new wine.

I will lie down in peace and sleep comes at once
for you alone, LORD, make me dwell in safety.

—*Psalm 4*

O Lord Jesus, king of bliss
How shall I be set at rest?
Who shall teach me and tell me
	what I need to know
if I cannot at this time see it in you?

   —*Julian of Norwich, fourteenth century*

When I lie down I say, 'When shall I rise?'
	But the night is long,
	and I am full of tossing until dawn.

   —*Job 7:4*

Be present, O merciful God, and protect us through the hours of this night, so that we who are wearied by the changes and chances of this life may rest in your eternal changelessness; through Jesus Christ our Lord.

—*Book of Common Prayer*

May nothing disturb you
nothing affright you;
everything will pass,
God never changes.
Patience
attains all;
whoever has God
lacks nothing;
only God suffices.

—*attributed to Saint Teresa of Avila, sixteenth century*

You who live in the shelter of the Most High
    who abide in the shadow of the Almighty,
will say to the LORD, "My refuge
      and my fortress;
    my God, in whom I trust!"

You will not fear the terror of the night,
    or the arrow that flies by day,
or the pestilence that stalks in darkness,
or the destruction that wastes at noonday.

Those who love me, I will deliver;
    I will protect those who know my name.
When they call to me, I will answer them;
    I will be with them in trouble,
    I will rescue them and honor them.

—Psalm 91: 1–2, 5–6, 14–15

Father in heaven, when the thought of you wakes in our hearts, let it not wake like a frightened bird that flies about in dismay, but like a child waking from its sleep with a heavenly smile.

—*Søren Kierkegaard, nineteenth century*

Then Jesus made his disciples get into the boat and precede him to the other side toward Bethsaida, while he dismissed the crowd. And when he had taken leave of them, he went off to the mountain to pray. When it was evening, the boat was far out on the sea and he was alone on the shore. Then he saw that they were tossed about while rowing, for the wind was against them. About the fourth watch of the night, he came towards them walking on the sea. He meant to pass by them. But when they saw him walking on the sea, they thought it was a ghost and cried out. They had all seen him and were terrified. But at once he spoke with them, "Take courage, it is I, do not be afraid!" He got into the boat with them and the wind died down.

—*Mark 6:45–51*

For I am convinced that neither death, nor life, nor angels, nor rulers, nor things present, nor things to come, nor powers, nor height, nor depth, nor anything else in all creation, will be able to separate us from the love of God in Christ Jesus our Lord.

—*Romans 8:38–39*

I slept,
but my heart
was awake.

NIGHT WORK

I thought the earth
remembered me, she
took me back so tenderly, arranging
her dark skirts, her pockets
full of lichens and seeds. I slept
as never before, a stone
on the riverbed, nothing
between me and the white fire of the stars
but my thoughts, and they floated
light as moths among the branches
of the perfect trees. All night
I heard the small kingdoms breathing
around me, the insects, and the birds
who do their work in the darkness. All night
I rose and fell, as if in water, grappling
with a luminous doom. By morning
I had vanished at least a dozen times
into something better.

—*Mary Oliver*

Let my prayer be counted as incense before you,
    and the lifting up of my hands
        as an evening sacrifice.

—*Psalm 141:2*

O God, your unfailing providence sustains the
world we live in and the life we live: Watch over
those, both night and day, who work while
others sleep, and grant that we may never forget
that our common life depends upon each
other's toil; through Jesus Christ our Lord.

—*Book of Common Prayer*

Jesus said, "The kingdom of heaven will be like this. Ten bridesmaids took their lamps and went to meet the bridegroom. Five of them were foolish, and five were wise. When the foolish took their lamps, they took no oil with them; but the wise took flasks of oil with their lamps. As the bridegroom was delayed, all of them became drowsy and slept. But at midnight there was a shout, 'Look! Here is the bridegroom! Come out to meet him.' Then all those brides-maids got up and trimmed their lamps. The foolish said to the wise, 'Give us some of your oil, for our lamps are going out.' But the wise replied, 'No, there will not be enough for you and for us; you had better go to the dealers and buy some for yourselves.' And while they went to buy it, the bridegroom came, and those who were ready went with him into the wedding banquet; and the door was shut. Later the other bridesmaids came also, saying, 'Lord, lord, open to us.' But he replied, 'Truly I tell you, I do not know you.' Keep awake therefore, for you know neither the day nor the hour.'"

—*Matthew 25:1–13*

Peter, bound with two chains, was sleeping between two soldiers, while guards in front of the door were keeping watch over the prison. Suddenly an angel of the Lord appeared and a light shone in the cell. He tapped Peter on the side and woke him, saying, "Get up quickly."

—*Acts 12:6b–7*

Samuel was lying down in the temple of the LORD, where the ark of God was. Then the LORD called, "Samuel! Samuel!" and he said, "Here I am!" and ran to Eli, and said, "Here I am, for you called me." But he said, "I did not call; lie down again." So he went and lay down. The LORD called again, "Samuel!" Samuel got up and went to Eli, and said, "Here I am, for you called me." But he said, "I did not call, my son; lie down again." Now Samuel did not yet know the LORD, and the word of the LORD had not yet been revealed to him. The LORD called Samuel again, a third time. And he got up and went to Eli, and said,

"Here I am, for you called me." Then Eli perceived that the LORD was calling the boy. Therefore Eli said to Samuel, "Go, lie down; and if he calls you, you shall say, 'Speak, LORD, for your servant is listening.'" So Samuel went and lay down in his place.

Now the LORD came and stood there, calling as before, "Samuel! Samuel!" And Samuel said, "Speak, for your servant is listening."

—*1 Samuel 3:3b–10*

Come, bless the LORD, all you servants
    of the LORD,
  who stand by night in the house
    of the LORD!
Lift up your hands to the holy place,
  and bless the LORD.

May the LORD, maker of heaven and earth,
  bless you from Zion.

—*Psalm 134*

Stand up all night, except a small portion of it,
      for prayer:
Half; or curtail the half a little,—
Or add to it: And with measured tone
      intone the Koran,
Verily, at the oncoming of night
      are *devout* impressions strongest,
      and words are most collected.

   —*the Koran 73:2–4, 6*

At midnight I rise to praise you,
      because of your righteous ordinances.

   —*Psalm 119:62*

Waking in the night for prayer does prepare
you for other disruptions in time and routine.
If you are used to turning your attention
toward Christ whenever you rise, then when
the call comes to be at the bedside of a dying
friend or to rescue a stranded daughter when
her car breaks down, the prayer you have
developed precedes your response.

—*Suzanne Guthrie*

During the night an angel of the Lord opened
the prison doors, brought the apostles out, and
said, "Go, stand in the temple and tell the
people the whole message about this life."

—*Acts 5:19–20*

We begin praying when we have urgent, if generally unimportant, needs and, when talking to God has become habitual, we gradually grow aware of our faults and our even more pressing need for forgiveness, until God's great mercies and goodness and faithfulness loom so hugely in our consciousness that we are in awe and whatever else we formerly did in prayer seems empty. Mystics often find intense gratification in merely being in the presence of the Holy One, their souls singing God's praise.

—*Ron Hansen*

Soul of Christ, sanctify me.
Body of Christ, heal me.
Blood of Christ, drench me.
Water from the side of Christ, wash me.
Passion of Christ, strengthen me.

Good Jesus, hear me.

In your wounds shelter me.
From turning away keep me.
From the evil one protect me.
At the hour of my death call me.
Into your presence lead me,
to praise you with all your saints
for ever and ever.

—*Anima Christi, fourteenth century*

To pray is to take notice of the wonder, to regain the sense of the mystery that animates all beings, the divine margin in all attainments. Prayer is our humble answer to the inconceivable surprise of living. It is all we can offer in return for the mystery by which we live.

—*Rabbi Heschel, twentieth century*

On a dark night
 Kindled in love with yearnings—
 Oh, happy chance!—
 I went forth unobserved,
 My house being now at rest.
  —Saint John of the Cross

How does one hush one's house,
each proud possessive wall, each sighing rafter,
the rooms made restless
        with remembered laughter
or wounding echoes, the permissive doors,
the stairs that vacillate from up to down,
windows that bring in color and event

from countryside or town,
oppressive ceilings and complaining floors?

The house must first of all accept the night.
Let it erase the walls and their display,
impoverish the rooms till they are filled
with humble silences; let clocks be stilled
and all the selfish urgencies of day.

Midnight is not the time to greet a guest.
Caution the doors against both foes and friends,
and try to make the windows understand
their unimportance when the daylight ends.
Persuade the stairs to patience, and deny
the passages their aimless to and fro.
Virtue it is that puts a house at rest.
How well repaid that tenant is, how blest
who, when the call is heard,
is free to take his kindled heart and go.

—*Jessica Powers, twentieth century*

I slept, but my heart was awake.
Listen! my beloved is knocking.

—*Song of Solomon 5:2*

One dark night,
fired with love's urgent longings
—ah, the sheer grace!—
I went out unseen,
my house being now all stilled.

On that glad night
in secret, for no one saw me,
nor did I look at anything
with no other light or guide
than the one that burned in my heart.

This guided me
more surely than the light of noon
to where he was awaiting me
—him I knew so well—
there in a place where no one appeared.

O guiding night!
O night more lovely than the dawn!
O night that has united
    the Lover with his beloved,
transforming the beloved in her Lover.

I abandoned and forgot myself,
laying my face on my Beloved;
all things ceased; I went out from myself,
leaving my cares
forgotten among the lilies.

—*Saint John of the Cross, sixteenth century*

Some nights stay up till dawn,
as the moon sometimes does for the sun.
Be a full bucket pulled up the dark way
of a well, then lifted out into light.

—*Rumi, thirteenth century Persian mystic*

The seed is in the ground.
Now may we rest in hope
While darkness does its work.

—*Wendell Berry*

Now, Lord, you let your servant go in peace;
your word has been fulfilled;
my own eyes have seen the salvation
which you have prepared in the sight
    of every people:
a light to reveal you to the nations
and the glory of your people Israel.

—*Luke 2:29–32 (Nunc Dimitis)*

Deep peace, p. 18: *The New Book of Christian Prayers,* comp. by Tony Castle. New York: Crossroad, 1986.

Charm with, p. 18: "Advent" by Thomas Merton, from *Selected Poems of Thomas Merton,* copyright © 1946 by New Directions Publishing Corp. Reprinted by permission of New Directions Publishing Corp.

God of, pp. 19–20: *Prayers for Sundays and Seasons, Year C.* Chicago: Liturgy Training Publications, © 1997 Archdiocese of Chicago.

Lord of light, p. 23; Come, Lord, p. 25: *An African Prayer Book,* selected and with introductions by Desmond Tutu. New York: Doubleday: © 1995 by Desmond Tutu.

To go in, p. 24: "To Know the Dark," from *Collected Poems, 1957–1982* by Wendell Berry. Copyright © 1985 by Wendell Berry. Reprinted by permission of North Point Press, a division of Farrar, Straus and Giroux, LLC.

You darkness, that I come from, p. 24: from *Selected Poems of Rainer Maria Rilke,* edited and translated by Robert Bly. © 1981 by Robert Bly. Reprinted by permission of HarperCollins Publishers, Inc.

Lord Jesus, p. 26: *Hymn of the Universe,* by Pierre Teilhard de Chardin. English translation © 1965 by William Collins Sons & Co. Ltd., London and Harper & Row, Inc., New York. Originally published in French as L'Hymne de l'Univers © 1961 by Editions du Seuil. Reprinted by permission of Georges Borchardt, Inc., for Editions du Seuil.

All you, p. 26: In the *New Revised Standard Version* of the Bible. These verses may be found in the deuterocanonical book called The Prayer of Azariah and the Song of the Three Jews 1:39–41; 47–48.

Darkness we, p. 28: from *Words around the Fire.* Chicago: Liturgy Training Publications, © 1990 Archdiocese of Chicago.

Lord, this winter, pp. 29–30: "Prayer of Taking Stock," from *The Hour of the Unexpected.* Chicago: The Thomas More Press, copyright © 1992 by John Shea. All rights reserved.

Take my hand, pp. 31–32: copyright Warner Brothers, Incorporated. In *An African Prayerbook,* selected and with introductions by Desmond Tutu. New York: Doubleday, 1995.

A man, p. 32; and The seed, p. 56: *A Timbered Choir, the Sabbath Poems, 1979–1997.* Washington, D.C.: Counterpoint, © 1998 by Wendell Berry.

I said, p. 34: *The Cloister Walk.* New York: Riverhead Books, © 1996
by Kathleen Norris.

O Lord, p. 36: Reprinted with permission from *Praying with Julian of Norwich* by Ritamary Bradley. Copyright 1994; all rights reserved. Twenty-Third Publications, Mystic, Connecticut 06355.

May nothing, p. 37: *Oracional Bilingue, a Prayer Book for Spanish-English Communities,* ed. by Jorge Perales. Collegeville, Minnesota: The Liturgical Press, © 1994 The Order of St. Benedict.

Stand up, p. 48: *The Koran,* trans. from the Arabic by J. M. Rodwell. London: Everyman, J. M. Dent, 2001.

Waking in, p. 49: copyright © 2000 by Suzanne Guthrie. All rights reserved. Excerpt is reprinted from *Praying the Hours* by Suzanne Guthrie; published by Cowlie Publications, 907 Massachusetts Avenue, Cambridge, MA 02139. www.cowley.org (800-225-1534).

We begin, p. 50: passage from p. 174 from *A Stay Against Confusion: Essays on Faith and Fiction* by Ron Hansen. Copyright © 2001 by Ron Hansen. Reprinted by permission of HarperCollins Publishers, Inc.

To pray, p. 52: *Moral Grandeur and Spiritual Audacity: Essays,* ed. by Susannah Heschel. New York: Farrar, Straus and Giroux, 1996.

How does, p. 52: From *The Selected Poetry of Jessica Powers,* published by ICS Publications, Washington, D.C. All copyrights, Carmelite Monastery, Pewaukee, Wisconsin. Used with permission.

One dark, p. 54: from *The Collected Works of St. John of the Cross,* trans. by Kieran Kavanaugh and Otilio Rodriguez © 1979, 1991 by Washington Province of Discalced Carmelites, ICS Publications, 2131 Lincoln Road, N.E., Washington, D.C. 20002-1199 U.S.A.

Some nights, p. 55: *The Essential Rumi,* trans. by Coleman Barks. New York: HarperSanFrancisco, copyright © 1995 by Coleman Barks. All rights reserved.